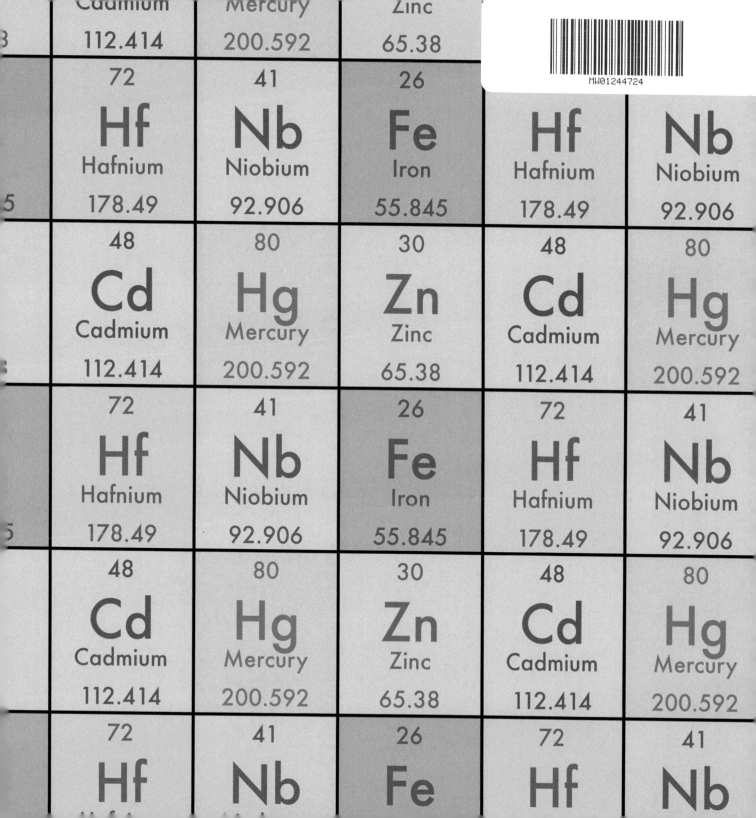

48	80	30
Cd	**Hg**	**Zn**
Cadmium	Mercury	Zinc
112.414	200.592	65.38
72	41	26
Hf	**Nb**	**Fe**
Hafnium	Niobium	Iron
178.49	92.906	55.845

This book belongs to:

_____

48	80	30
Cd	**Hg**	**Zn**
Cadmium	Mercury	Zinc
112.414	200.592	65.38
72	41	26
Hf	**Nb**	**Fe**
Hafnium	Niobium	Iron
178.49	92.906	55.845

About Transition Metals

Transition metals consists of the 38 chemical elements. These metals are mostly all hard, high-melting solids that can conduct heat and electricity well. Transition metals are less reactive and they lose electrons to form stable cations.

The Periodic Table of Elements

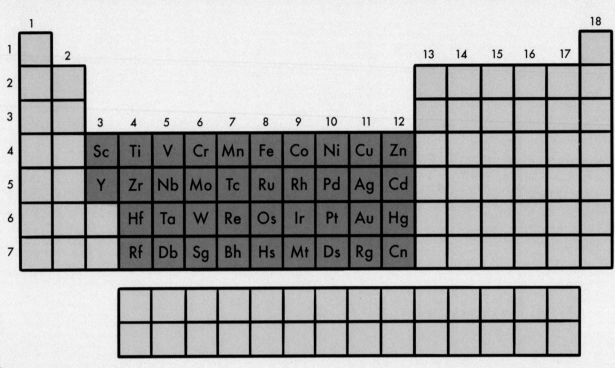

1		3	4	5	6	7	8	9	10	11	12	13	14	15	16	17	18
1	**2**																
		Sc	Ti	V	Cr	Mn	Fe	Co	Ni	Cu	Zn						
		Y	Zr	Nb	Mo	Tc	Ru	Rh	Pd	Ag	Cd						
		Hf	Ta	W	Re	Os	Ir	Pt	Au	Hg							
		Rf	Db	Sg	Bh	Hs	Mt	Ds	Rg	Cn							

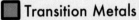

■ Transition Metals
□ Other Elements

The Periodic Table

Transition metals are a group of chemical elements from the d-block of the periodic table. Transition metals make up Groups 3-12 of the periodic table and they have at least 2 valence electrons.

Transition Metals History

Transition metals have been used since ancient Egypt. The name transition metal dates back to 1921 and it comes from what occurs in their valence electron shells.

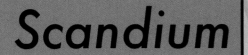

Scandium

Scandium is a chemical element and is a soft, light, silvery-white metal.

Scandium is considered non-toxic, but long term exposure can cause liver damage and respiratory diseases such as lung embolism.

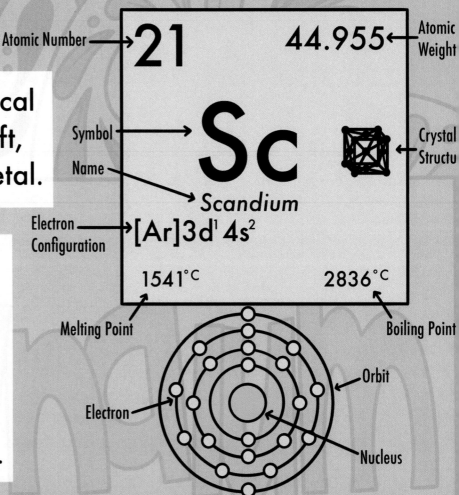

Atomic Number → 21

44.955 ← Atomic Weight

Symbol → Sc

Name → Scandium

Crystal Structu ←

Electron Configuration → [Ar]3d^1 4s^2

1541°C

2836°C

Melting Point

Boiling Point

Orbit

Electron

Nucleus

It can be used in aluminum-scandium alloys for aerospace industry components and for sports equipment. Scandium radionuclides has been identified in the late 1990s as promising for nuclear medicine applications.

Lars Nilson

Scandium was discovered in 1879 by the Swedish chemists Per Cleve and Lars Nilson.

Per Cleve

Scandium occurs in minute quantities in over 800 mineral species and is very widely distributed.

What contains scandium?

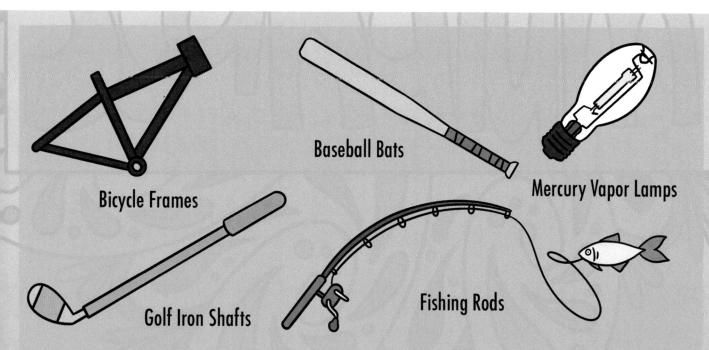

Bicycle Frames

Baseball Bats

Mercury Vapor Lamps

Golf Iron Shafts

Fishing Rods

Yttrium

Yttrium is a chemical element and is a silvery white, soft, ductile metal.

Yttrium toxicity can cause lung embolisms, especially during long-term exposure and cancer.

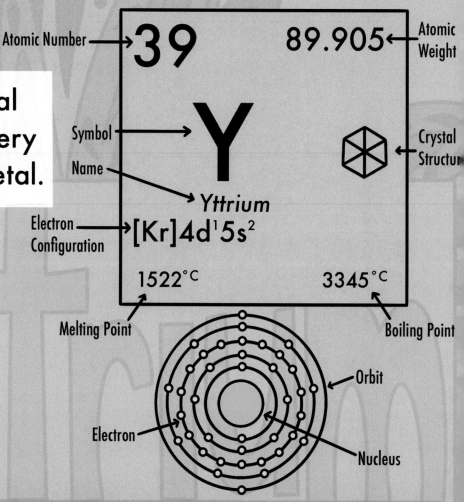

Atomic Number → 39   89.905 ← Atomic Weight

Symbol → **Y**

Name

Yttrium

Electron Configuration → $[Kr]4d^1 5s^2$

Crystal Structure

$1522°C$ $3345°C$

Melting Point   Boiling Point

Orbit

Electron

Nucleus

It can be used as an additive in alloys and it increases the strength of aluminium and magnesium alloys. Yttrium 90 can be used to help kill cancer cells. It is also used in medical lasers and biomedical implants.

Yttrium was discovered in 1794 by the Finnish chemist Johan Gadolin.

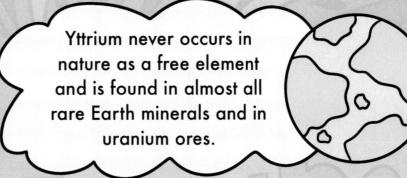

Yttrium never occurs in nature as a free element and is found in almost all rare Earth minerals and in uranium ores.

What contains yttrium?

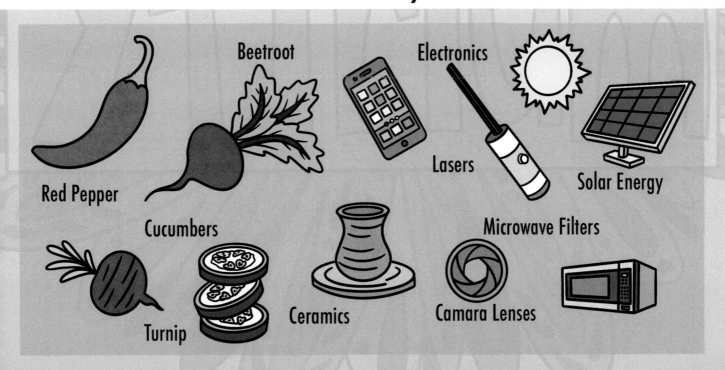

Red Pepper

Beetroot

Electronics

Lasers

Solar Energy

Cucumbers

Microwave Filters

Turnip

Ceramics

Camara Lenses

Titanium

Titanium is a chemical element and is a light, silvery-white, hard, metal.

Titanium toxicity can cause lung diseases, skin diseases, sinus congestion, cancer, and vision problems.

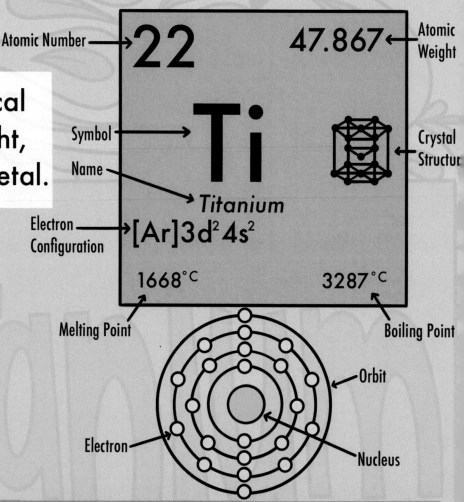

Atomic Number → 22

47.867 ← Atomic Weight

Symbol → Ti

Crystal Structur ←

Name → Titanium

Electron Configuration → [Ar]3d² 4s²

1668°C

3287°C

Melting Point

Boiling Point

Orbit

Electron

Nucleus

It can be used to manufacture laser electrodes, dental drills, and forceps. Titanium is used in implants, surgical devices, and pacemaker cases. It is most common in joint replacements and tooth implants.

Titanium was discovered in 1791 by the British mineralogist William Gregor.

Titanium is not found as a pure element in nature, but is always present in igneous rocks and the sediments derived from them.

What contains titanium?

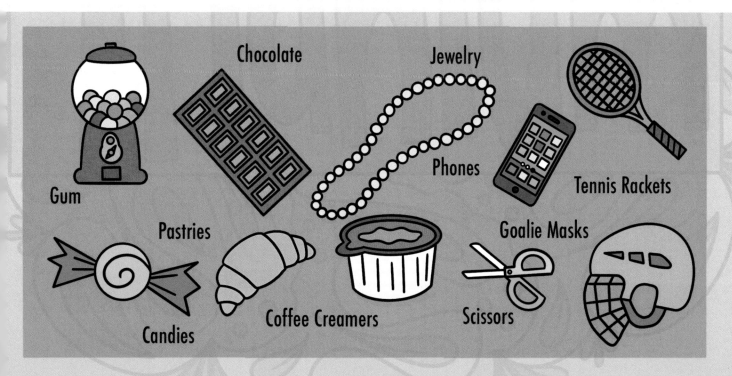

Gum

Chocolate

Jewelry

Phones

Tennis Rackets

Pastries

Goalie Masks

Coffee Creamers

Scissors

Candies

Zirconium

Zirconium is a chemical element and is a silver-gray and ductile metal.

Zirconium toxicity can cause vomiting, hypotension, headaches, nausea, eye irritations, blurred vision, and conjunctivitis.

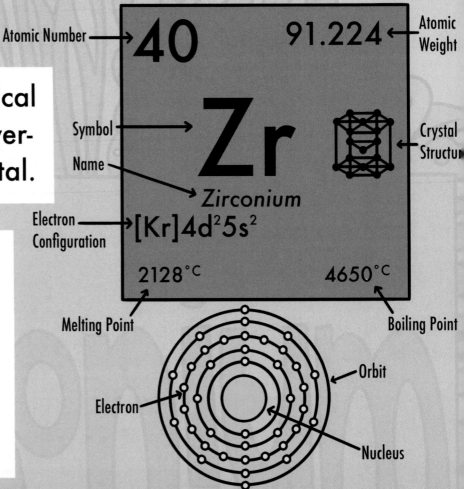

Atomic Number → 40   91.224 ← Atomic Weight

Symbol → Zr ← Crystal Structure

Name → Zirconium

Electron Configuration → [Kr]4d^{2}5s^2

2128°C   4650°C

Melting Point   Boiling Point

Orbit

Electron

Nucleus

It can be used to make crucibles that will withstand heat-shock, furnace linings, foundry bricks, and abrasives. Zirconium is used in medicine as a potassium binder, which helps treat hyperkalemia.

Zirconium was discovered in 1789 by the German chemist Martin Klaproth.

Zirconium occurs in a variety of rock types and geologic environments, but it's most often in igneous rocks in the form of zircon.

What contains zirconium?

Plum

Pineapple

Watermelon

Grapes

Lemon

Glass

Deodorant

Cranberries

Cherries

Artificial Gemstones

Hafnium

Hafnium is a chemical element and is a silver-gray and lustrous metal.

Hafnium has no known toxicity, but overexposure can cause cause mild irritation of the eyes, skin, and mucous membranes.

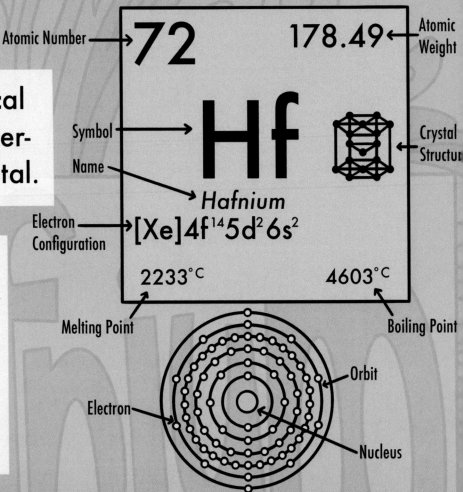

Atomic Number → 72

178.49 ← Atomic Weight

Symbol → Hf

Crystal Structure

Name → Hafnium

Electron Configuration → [Xe]4f^{14}5d^{2}6s^2

2233°C

4603°C

Melting Point

Boiling Point

Orbit

Electron

Nucleus

It is a good absorber of neutrons and it can be used to make control rods, such as those found in nuclear reactors and nuclear submarines. Hafnium has a very high melting point and is used in plasma welding torches.

George Hevesy

Dirk Coster

Hafnium was discovered in 1923 by the Dutch physicist Dirk Coster and the Hungarian radiochemist George Hevesy.

Hafnium is rarely found free in nature. It is instead present in most zirconium minerals at a concentration of up to 5%.

What contains hafnium?

Lightbulbs

Ceramics

Space Rocket Engines

Rutherfordium

Rutherfordium is a radioactive synthetic chemical element.

Rutherfordium is expected to be harmful to living organisms because of its radioactivity.

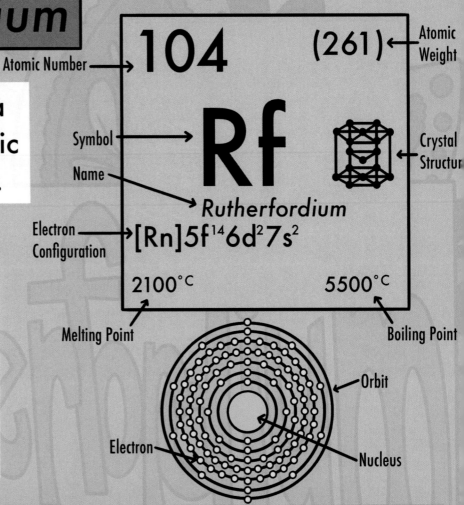

Atomic Number → **104**

(261) ← Atomic Weight

Symbol → **Rf**

Crystal Structure

Name → *Rutherfordium*

Electron Configuration → $[Rn]5f^{14}6d^{2}7s^{2}$

2100°C

5500°C

Melting Point

Boiling Point

Orbit

Electron

Nucleus

It is named after the New Zealand Chemist Ernest Rutherford, who was one of the first people to explain the structure of atoms. Rutherfordium is created by bombarding californium^{-249} with carbon^{-12} nuclei.

Rutherfordium was discovered in 1964 by the American nuclear scientist Albert Ghiorso.

Rutherfordium does not occur naturally on Earth and it is only produced in a lab.

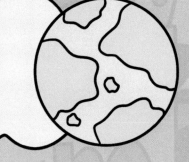

What contains rutherfordium?

Nothing

- Due to the small amounts produced, its short half-life, instability, and rarity, there are currently no commercial applications using rutherfordium.
- Rutherfordium has been used for scientific research purposes only.

Vanadium

Vanadium is a chemical element and is a hard and silvery-grey metal.

Vanadium toxicity can cause cramps, nausea, headache, tremors, dizziness, diarrhea, vomiting, and weight reduction.

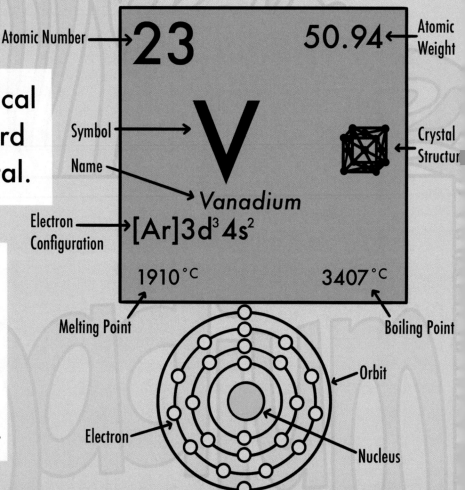

Atomic Number → 23

50.94 ← Atomic Weight

Symbol → V

Crystal Structur ←

Name → Vanadium

Electron Configuration → [Ar]$3d^3 4s^2$

1910°C

3407°C

Melting Point

Boiling Point

Orbit

Electron

Nucleus

It can be used in the process of refining uranium for nuclear purposes and it is a substitute for molybdenum in armor steel. Vanadium is used to treat diabetes, low blood sugar, high cholesterol, heart disease, and helps prevent cancer.

Vanadium was discovered in 1801 by the Spanish scientist Andrés Manuel del Río.

Vanadium occurs naturally in about 65 minerals and significant concentrations are found in certain coal and oil deposits.

What contains vanadium?

Mushrooms

Black Pepper

Beer

Grain

Wine

Nuclear Reactors

Tools

Shellfish

Parsley

Dill Weed

Niobium

Niobium is a chemical element and is a shiny, white, ductile metal.

Niobium has no reports of humans being poisoned by it, but it can cause eye and skin irritation.

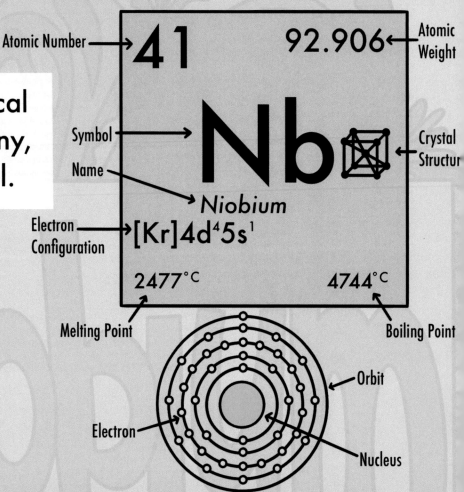

Atomic Number → 41

92.906 ← Atomic Weight

Symbol → **Nb**

Crystal Structur

Name → *Niobium*

Electron Configuration → [Kr]4d⁴5s¹

2477°C

Melting Point

4744°C

Boiling Point

Orbit

Electron

Nucleus

It can be used in alloys including stainless steel and it helps improves the strength of alloys, particularly at low temperatures. Niobium is used in pacemakers and has been used in trials studying the treatment of obesity.

Niobium was discovered in 1801 by the British mineralogist Charles Hatchett.

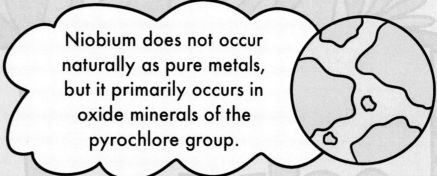

Niobium does not occur naturally as pure metals, but it primarily occurs in oxide minerals of the pyrochlore group.

What contains niobium?

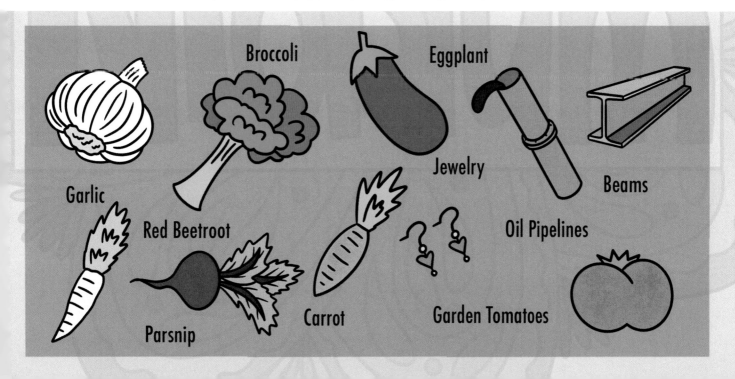

Broccoli

Eggplant

Garlic

Jewelry

Beams

Red Beetroot

Oil Pipelines

Carrot

Garden Tomatoes

Parsnip

Tantalum

Tantalum is a chemical element and is a rare, shiny, gray, dense metal.

Tantalum has low toxicity because they are poorly absorbed and quickly eliminated from mammals, but it may cause skin or eye irritations.

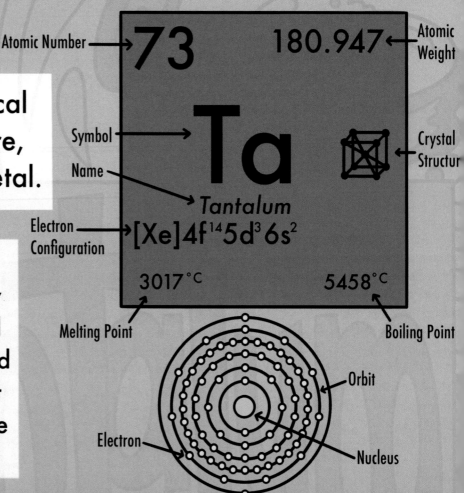

Atomic Number → 73

180.947 ← Atomic Weight

Symbol → Ta

Crystal Structure

Name → Tantalum

Electron Configuration → $[Xe]4f^{14}5d^{3}6s^{2}$

3017°C

Melting Point

5458°C

Boiling Point

Orbit

Electron

Nucleus

It can be used in a variety of alloys to add high strength, ductility, and a high melting point. It is also one of the main uses in the production of electronic components. Tantalum is used in medical devices such as heart pacemakers.

Tantalum was discovered in 1802 by the Swedish analytical chemist Anders Gustaf Ekeberg.

Tantalum is only rarely found uncombined in nature, and it is mainly found in Australia, Brazil, Thailand, and Portugal.

What contains tantalum?

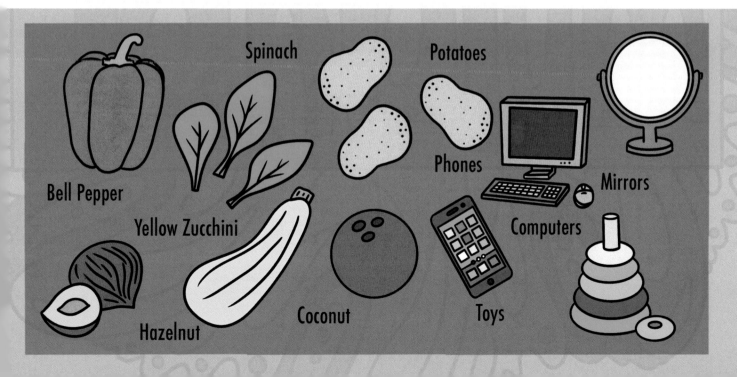

Bell Pepper

Spinach

Potatoes

Phones

Mirrors

Yellow Zucchini

Computers

Hazelnut

Coconut

Toys

Dubnium

Dubnium is a highly radioactive synthetic chemical element.

Dubnium is expected to be harmful to living organisms because of its radioactivity.

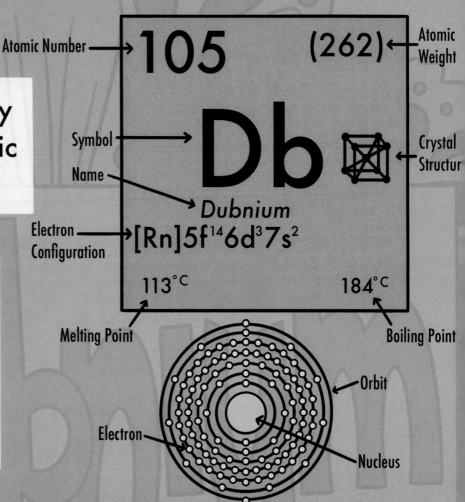

Atomic Number → 105

(262) ← Atomic Weight

Symbol → Db

← Crystal Structur

Name → Dubnium

Electron Configuration → [Rn]5f^{14}6d^{3}7s^2

113°C

184°C

Melting Point

Boiling Point

Orbit

Electron

Nucleus

Dubnium has 7 recognized isotopes. The most stable isotope is dubnium^{-268}, and it has a half-life of about 28 hours. It is named for Dubna, Russia, which is home of the Joint Institute for Nuclear Research, where the element was first reported.

Dubnium was discovered in 1967 by the American nuclear scientist Albert Ghiorso.

Dubnium does not occur naturally on Earth and it is only produced in a lab.

What contains dubnium?

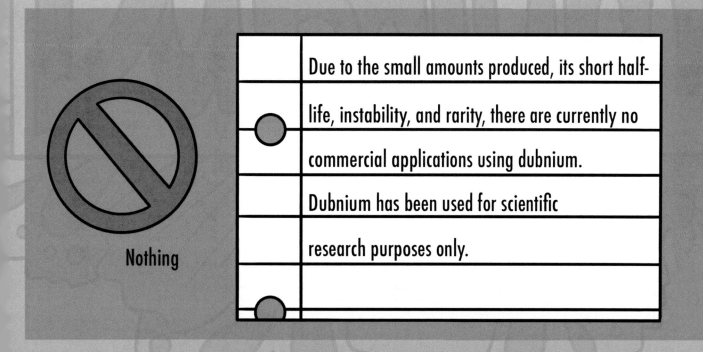

Nothing

○ Due to the small amounts produced, its short half-life, instability, and rarity, there are currently no commercial applications using dubnium.

Dubnium has been used for scientific research purposes only.

Chromium

Chromium is a chemical element and is a steely-grey and hard metal.

Chromium toxicity can cause pulmonary sensitization. It also increases the risk of lung, nasal, and sinus cancer.

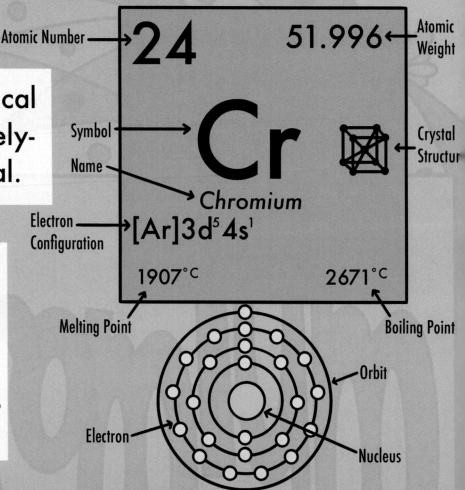

Atomic Number → 24

51.996 ← Atomic Weight

Symbol → Cr

Crystal Structur

Name → Chromium

Electron Configuration → [Ar]3d^{5}4s^1

1907°C

2671°C

Melting Point

Boiling Point

Orbit

Electron

Nucleus

It can be used to harden steel, manufacture stainless steel, and produce several alloys. Chromium can be medically used for diabetes, high cholesterol, athletic performance, and bipolar disorder.

Chromium was discovered in 1797 by the French chemist Louis Nicolas Vauquelin.

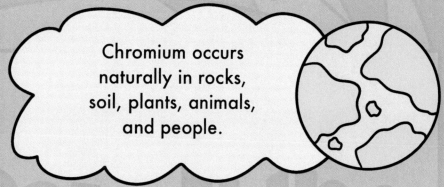

Chromium occurs naturally in rocks, soil, plants, animals, and people.

What contains chromium?

Butter

Meat

Anchovy

Shrimp

Brazil Nuts

Cabbage

Salt

Apples

Brussel Sprouts

Paint

Molybdenum

Molybdenum is a chemical element and is a silvery-white metal.

Molybdenum toxicity can cause poor growth, infertility, diarrhea, lameness, ataxia, and osteoporosis.

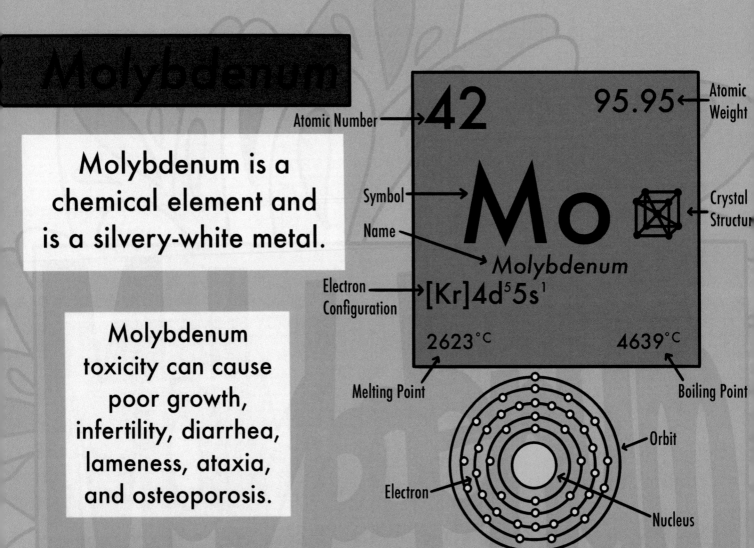

Atomic Number →42

95.95← Atomic Weight

Symbol → Mo

Crystal Structure

Name → Molybdenum

Electron Configuration → [Kr]4d^{5}5s^1

2623°C

4639°C

Melting Point

Boiling Point

Orbit

Electron

Nucleus

It can be used in steel alloys to increase strength, hardness, electrical conductivity, and resistance to corrosion and wear. Molybdenum is medically used for treating arthritis, cancer, and neuropsychiatric disorders.

Molybdenum was discovered in 1778 by the Swedish pharmacist Carl Wilhelm Scheele.

Molybdenum does not occur naturally as a free metal on Earth, but it is found in various oxidation states in minerals.

What contains molybdenum?

Pumpkins

Lima Beans

Cheese

Milk

Milk

Bananas

Corn

Eggs

Lettuce

Soybeans

Yogurt

Tungsten

Tungsten is a chemical element and is a greyish-white lustrous metal.

Tungsten toxicity can cause lung fibrosis, eye irritations, nose irritations, coughs, memory problems, headaches, nausea, and seizures.

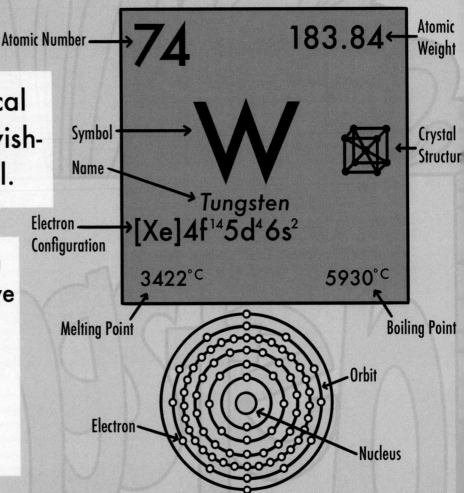

Atomic Number → 74

183.84 ← Atomic Weight

Symbol → **W**

Crystal Structure

Name → Tungsten

Electron Configuration → $[Xe]4f^{14}5d^{4}6s^{2}$

3422°C

5930°C

Melting Point

Boiling Point

Orbit

Electron

Nucleus

It can be used in heavy metal alloys such as high speed steel, from which cutting tools are manufactured. It is also used in electrodes, heating elements, and field emitters. Tungsten is used medically for radioactive source containers.

Juan Elhuyar

Tungsten was discovered in 1783 by the Spanish chemists Fausto Elhuyar and Juan Elhuyar.

Fausto Elhuyar
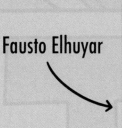

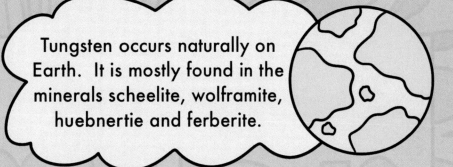
Tungsten occurs naturally on Earth. It is mostly found in the minerals scheelite, wolframite, huebnertie and ferberite.

What contains tungsten?

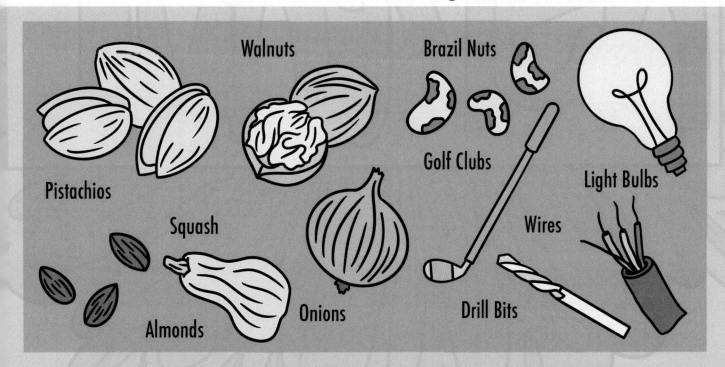

Pistachios

Walnuts

Brazil Nuts

Golf Clubs

Light Bulbs

Squash

Wires

Almonds

Onions

Drill Bits

Seaborgium

Seaborgium is a radioactive synthetic chemical element.

Seaborgium is expected to be harmful to living organisms because of its radioactivity.

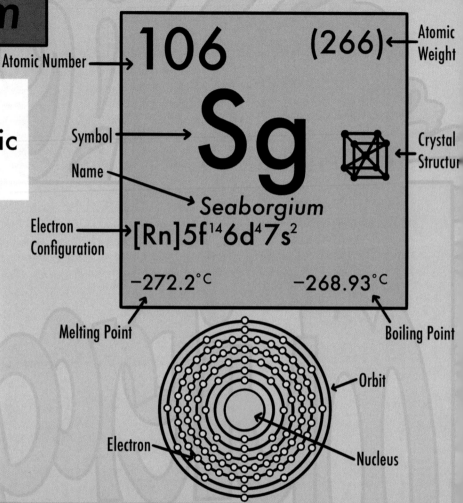

Atomic Number → 106

(266) ← Atomic Weight

Symbol → **Sg**

Name → *Seaborgium*

Electron Configuration → $[Rn]5f^{14}6d^{4}7s^{2}$

Crystal Structure

−272.2°C

−268.93°C

Melting Point

Boiling Point

Orbit

Electron

Nucleus

It is named after the American nuclear chemist Glenn T. Seaborg, who was instrumental in producing several transuranium elements. Seaborgium is created by bombarding californium $^{-249}$ with oxygen $^{-18}$ nuclei.

Seaborgium was discovered in 1974 by the American nuclear scientist Albert Ghiorso.

Seaborgium does not occur naturally on Earth and it is only produced in a lab.

What contains seaborgium?

Nothing

○ Due to the small amounts produced, its short half-life, instability, and rarity, there are currently no commercial applications using seaborgium.

○ Seaborgium has been used for scientific research purposes only.

Manganese

Manganese is a chemical element and is a hard and silvery-grey metal.

Manganese toxicity can cause neurological disorders with symptoms that include tremors, difficulty walking, and facial muscle spasms.

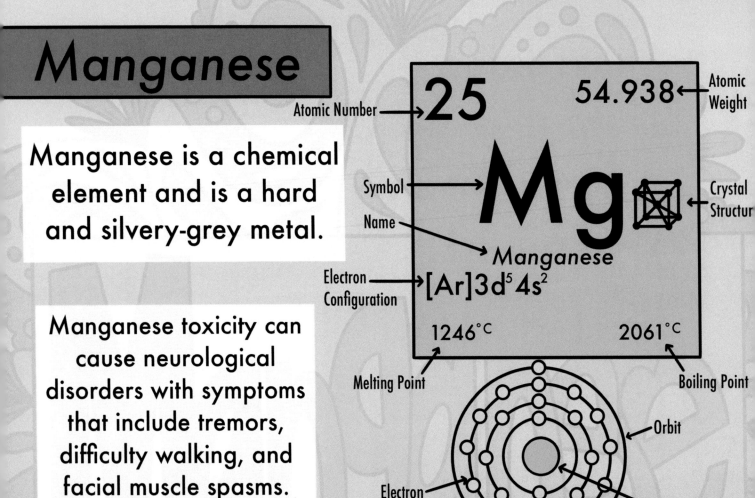

Atomic Number → 25

54.938 ← Atomic Weight

Symbol →

Mg

Crystal Structur

Name →

Manganese

Electron Configuration → [Ar]3d^{5}4s^2

1246°C

2061°C

Melting Point

Boiling Point

Orbit

Electron

Nucleus

It can be used to desulfurize and deoxidize steel in steel production and reduce the octane rating in gasoline. Manganese is used to protect the skin from oxygen-related and UV-related damage and help balance blood sugar levels naturally.

Manganese was discovered in 1774 by the Swedish chemist Johan Gottlieb Gahn.

Manganese does not occur on its own, but it is naturally found in a variety of minerals like manganite and pyrolusite.

What contains manganese?

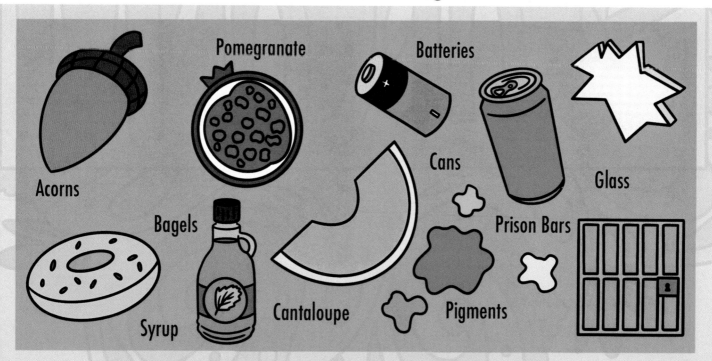

Acorns

Pomegranate

Batteries

Cans

Glass

Bagels

Prison Bars

Syrup

Cantaloupe

Pigments

Technetium

Technetium is a chemical element and is a silvery-gray radioactive metal.

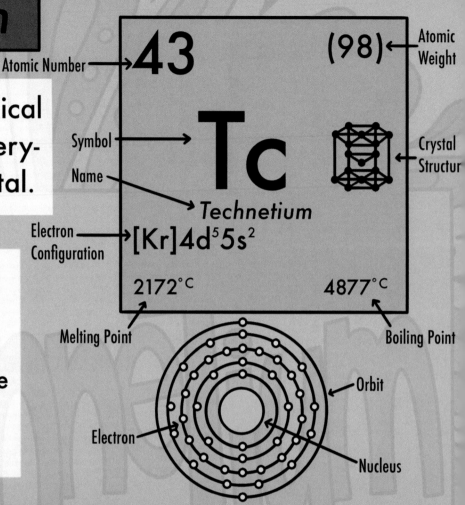

Atomic Number → **43**

(98) ← Atomic Weight

Symbol → **Tc**

Crystal Structur ←

Name → *Technetium*

Electron Configuration → $[Kr]4d^5 5s^2$

2172°C

4877°C

Melting Point

Boiling Point

Orbit

Electron

Nucleus

Technetium toxicity can cause rash, angioedema, fever, and anaphylaxis due to hypersensitivity reactions.

It can be used in a number of medical diagnostic imaging scans and in radioactive tracers. Technetium was the first artificially produced element, it was created by bombarding molybdenum with a stream of neutrons.

Technetium was discovered in 1937 by the Italian-American physicist Emilio Gino Segrè.

Technetium has been found in tiny quantities and it occurs naturally in the Earth's crust in minute concentrations of about 0.003 parts per trillion.

What contains technetium?

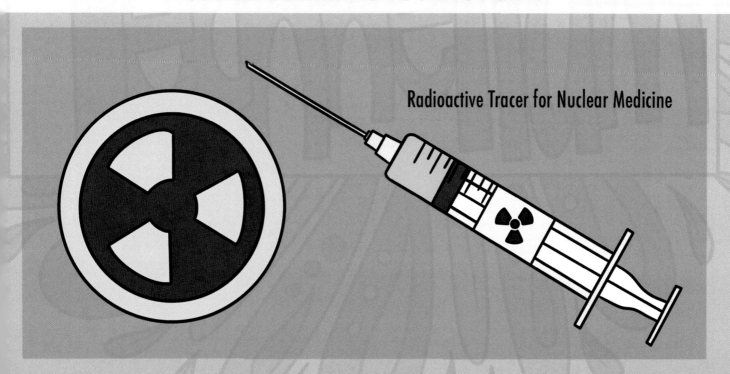

Radioactive Tracer for Nuclear Medicine

Rhenium

Rhenium is a chemical element and is a silvery-white and hard metal.

Little is known about rhenium toxicity and its compounds because it is used in very small amounts, but it may cause eye and skin irritations.

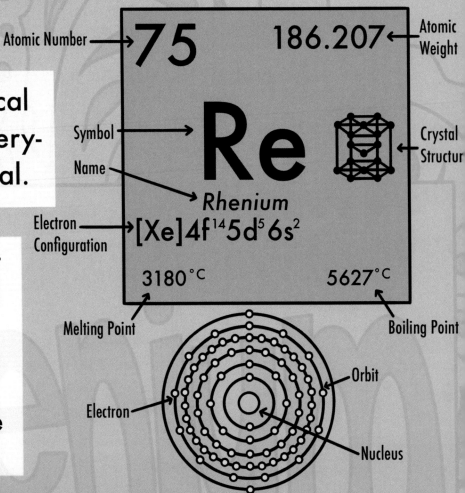

Atomic Number → 75

186.207 ← Atomic Weight

Symbol → Re

Crystal Structure

Name → Rhenium

Electron Configuration → $[Xe]4f^{14}5d^{5}6s^{2}$

3180 °C

5627 °C

Melting Point

Boiling Point

Orbit

Electron

Nucleus

It can be used as an additive to tungsten- and molybdenum-based alloys to give useful properties. Rhenium-186-HEDP is commonly used in Europe for the palliative treatment of bone pain from skeletal metastases.

Ida Noddack

Walter Noddack

Otto Berg

Rhenium was discovered in 1925 by the German chemists Walter Noddack, Ida Noddack, and Otto Berg.

Rhenium does not occur free in nature, but it is widely distributed in small amounts in other minerals.

What contains rhenium?

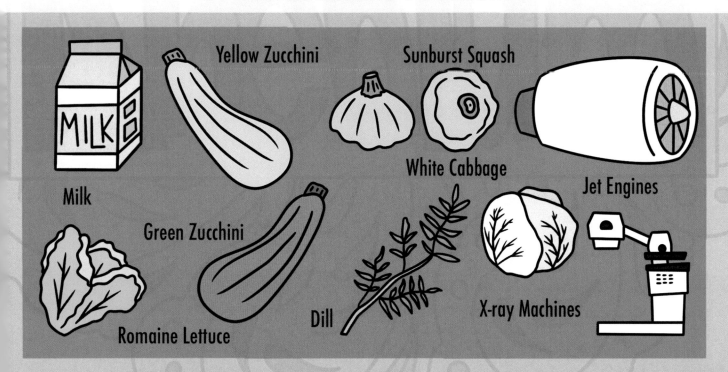

Milk

Yellow Zucchini

Green Zucchini

Romaine Lettuce

Sunburst Squash

White Cabbage

Dill

X-ray Machines

Jet Engines

Bohrium

Bohrium is a highly radioactive synthetic chemical element.

Bohrium is expected to be harmful to living organisms because of its radioactivity.

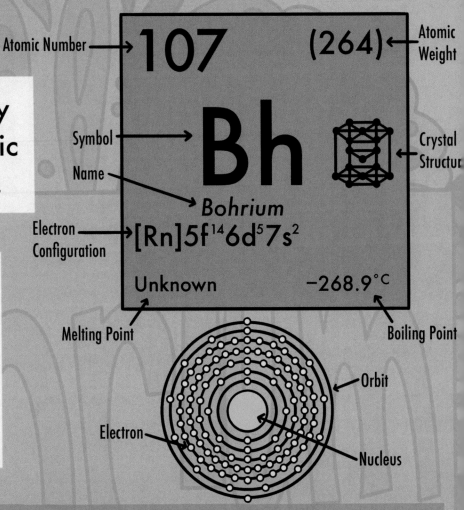

Atomic Number → 107 (264) ← Atomic Weight

Symbol → **Bh** → Crystal Structure

Name → *Bohrium*

Electron Configuration → $[Rn]5f^{14}6d^{5}7s^{2}$

Unknown $-268.9°C$

Melting Point   Boiling Point

Orbit

Electron

Nucleus

Bohrium is created by bombarding bismuth^{-204} with heavy nuclei of chromium^{-54}. It is named after the Danish physicist Niels Bohr to honor his contributions to the field of atomic science. It's most stable isotope has a half life of 17 seconds.

Gottfried
Münzenberg

Bohrium was discovered in 1981 by the German physics Peter Armbruster and Gottfried Münzenberg.

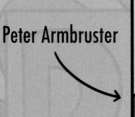

Peter Armbruster

Bohrium does not occur naturally on Earth and it is only produced in a lab.

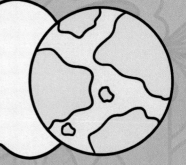

What contains bohrium?

Nothing

○	Due to the small amounts produced, its short half-life, instability, and rarity, there are currently no commercial applications using bohrium.
	Bohrium has been used for scientific research purposes only.
○	

Iron

Iron is a chemical element and is a shiny and metallic metal.

Iron toxicity can cause cancer, irregular heartbeat, cirrhosis of the liver, diabetes, darkening of the skin, abnormal heart rhythm, and arthritis.

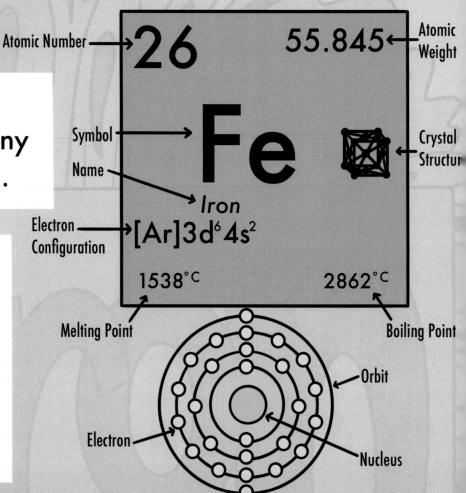

Atomic Number → 26   55.845 ← Atomic Weight

Symbol → Fe

Crystal Structur ←

Name → Iron

Electron Configuration → $[Ar]3d^6 4s^2$

1538°C   2862°C

Melting Point   Boiling Point

Orbit ←

Electron →

→ Nucleus

It can be used to make alloy steels like carbon steels with additives such as nickel, chromium, vanadium, tungsten, and manganese. Iron is used to treat or prevent anemia when the amount of iron taken in from the diet is not enough.

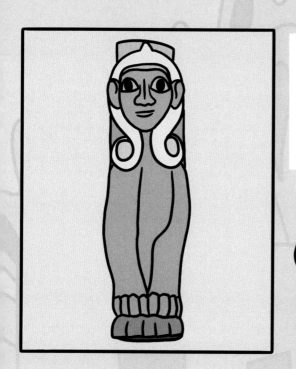

Iron was discovered between 5000 and 3000 BCE by the Hittites of ancient Egypt.

Iron is found distributed in the soil in low concentrations and is believed to be the major component of the Earth's core.

What contains iron?

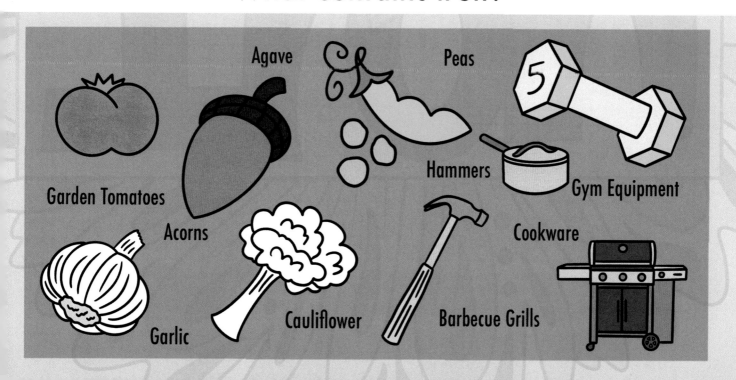

Agave

Peas

5

Garden Tomatoes

Hammers

Gym Equipment

Acorns

Cookware

Garlic

Cauliflower

Barbecue Grills

Ruthenium

Ruthenium is a chemical element and is a silvery-gray and hard metal.

Ruthenium toxicity can cause skin irritations and it may be irritating to the mucous membranes and upper respiratory tract.

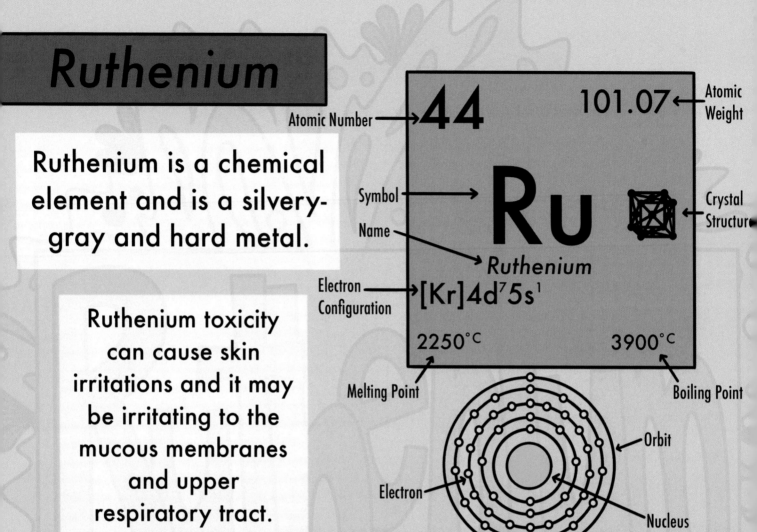

Atomic Number → 44

Atomic Weight → 101.07

Symbol → Ru

Name → Ruthenium

Electron Configuration → [Kr]4d⁷5s¹ $[Kr]4d^7 5s^1$

Crystal Structure

Melting Point — 2250°C

Boiling Point — 3900°C

Orbit

Electron

Nucleus

It can be used to coat the anodes of electrochemical cells for chlorine production. Ruthenium is used in catalysts for ammonia and acetic acid production and is used in solar cells, which turn light energy into electrical energy.

Ruthenium was discovered in 1844 by the German-Russian chemist Karl Ernst Claus.

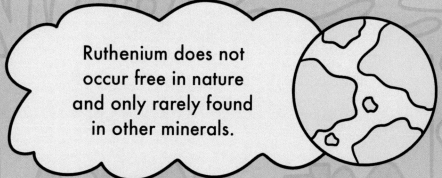

Ruthenium does not occur free in nature and only rarely found in other minerals.

What contains ruthenium?

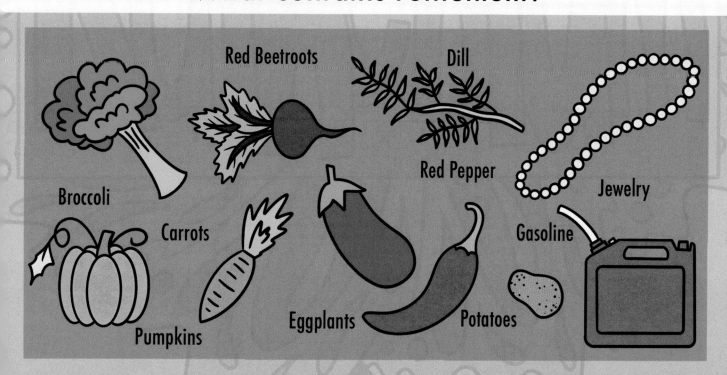

Broccoli

Red Beetroots

Dill

Red Pepper

Jewelry

Carrots

Pumpkins

Eggplants

Potatoes

Gasoline

Osmium

Osmium is a chemical element and is a gray-white and hard metal.

Osmium toxicity can cause irreversible eye damage like blindness and long-term exposure can cause damage to the liver and kidney.

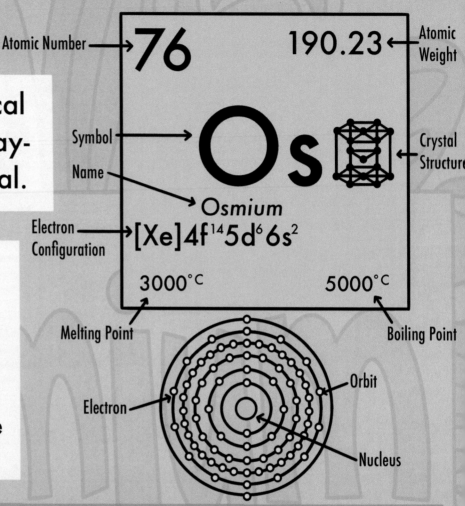

Atomic Number → 76

190.23 ← Atomic Weight

Symbol → Os

Crystal Structure

Name → Osmium

Electron Configuration → $[Xe]4f^{14}5d^6 6s^2$

3000°C

5000°C

Melting Point

Boiling Point

Orbit

Electron

Nucleus

It can be used in the chemical industry as a catalyst. Osmium is used to make surgical instruments and pacemakers. The name osmium is derived from the Greek word 'osme', which means smell.

Osmium was discovered in 1803 by the English chemist Smithson Tennant.

Osmium is the rarest of all stable elements and it occurs naturally as either a free element or in naturally occurring alloys.

What contains osmium?

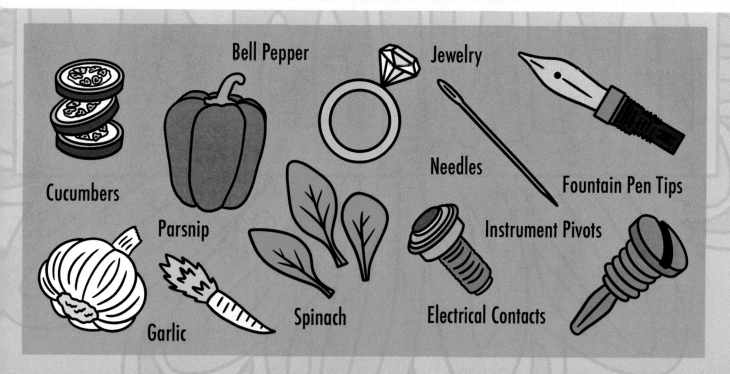

Cucumbers

Bell Pepper

Jewelry

Needles

Fountain Pen Tips

Parsnip

Instrument Pivots

Garlic

Spinach

Electrical Contacts

Hassium

Hassium is a highly radioactive synthetic chemical element.

Hassium is expected to be harmful to living organisms because of its radioactivity.

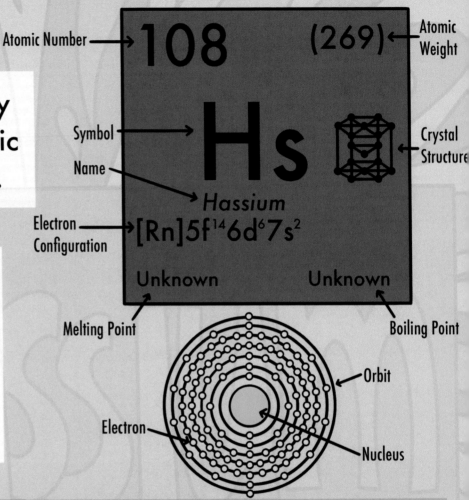

Atomic Number → 108 (269) ← Atomic Weight

Symbol → **Hs**

Name → *Hassium*

Electron Configuration → [Rn]$5f^{14}6d^{6}7s^{2}$

Unknown — Melting Point

Unknown — Boiling Point

Crystal Structure

Orbit

Electron

Nucleus

Hassium is created by bombarding curium^{-248} with energetic magnesium^{-26} ions. It is derived from the German state Hesse where Hassium was first made. It's most stable isotope is hassium^{-277} and it has a half life of around 12 minutes.

Gottfried Münzenberg

Peter Armbruster

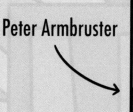

Hassium was discovered in 1984 by the German physics Peter Armbruster and Gottfried Münzenberg.

Hassium does not occur naturally on Earth and it is only produced in a lab.

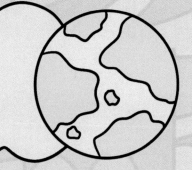

What contains hassium?

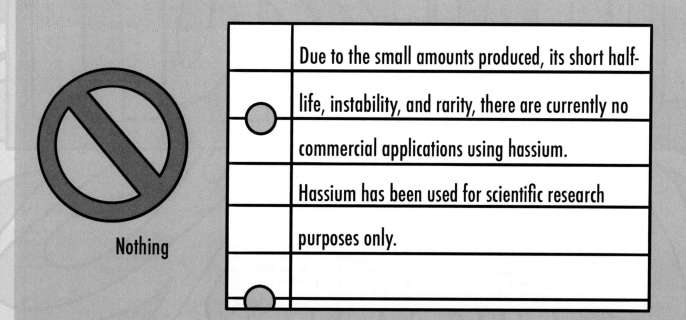

Nothing

○ Due to the small amounts produced, its short half-life, instability, and rarity, there are currently no commercial applications using hassium.

Hassium has been used for scientific research purposes only.

Cobalt

Cobalt is a chemical element and is a silvery-blue and brittle metal.

Cobalt toxicity can cause cardiomyopathy, deafness, nerve problems, ringing in the ears, thickening of the blood, and vision problems.

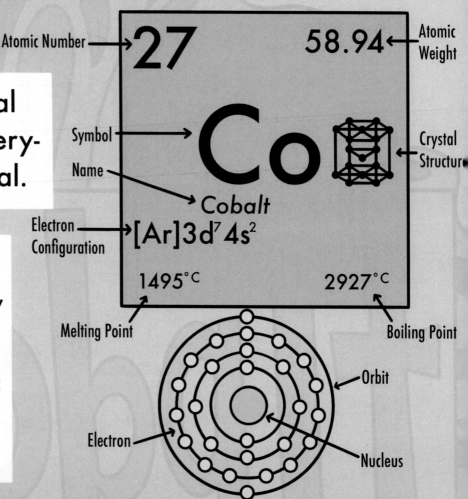

Atomic Number → 27   58.94 ← Atomic Weight

Symbol → Co ← Crystal Structure

Name → Cobalt

Electron Configuration → $[Ar]3d^7 4s^2$

1495°C   2927°C

Melting Point   Boiling Point

Orbit

Electron

Nucleus

It can be used to make airbags in automobiles and catalysts for the petroleum and chemical industries. Cobalt is medically used for radiation therapy as implants and as an external source of radiation exposure.

Cobalt was discovered in 1735 by the Swedish chemist Georg Brandt.

Cobalt is not found as a free element, but is found in the minerals cobaltite, skutterudite and erythrite.

What contains cobalt?

Milk

Apples

Fennel

Cosmetics

Buttons

Bricks

Glass

Turnip

Corn

Fenugreek

Rhodium

Rhodium is a chemical element and is a silver-white and metallic metal.

Rhodium toxicity may eye and skin irritations, but there are no reported cases of humans being affected by this element in any way.

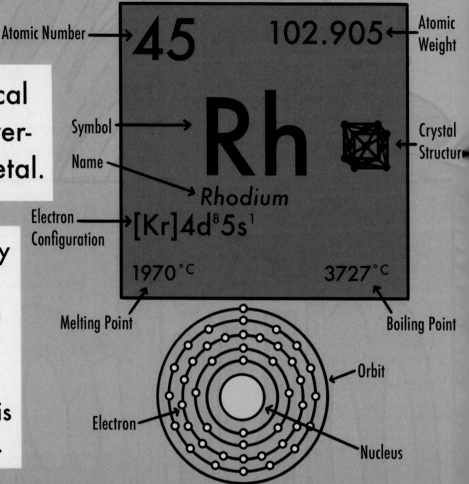

Atomic Number → 45   102.905 ← Atomic Weight

Symbol → Rh

Name → Rhodium

Crystal Structure

Electron Configuration → [Kr]4d⁸5s¹

1970°C   3727°C

Melting Point   Boiling Point

Orbit

Electron

Nucleus

It can be used as a catalyst in the making of nitric acid, acetic acid, and hydrogenation reactions. Rhodium is used in catalytic converters for cars and is responsible for the absorption of zirconium, molybdenum, and neodymium.

Rhodium was discovered in 1803 by the English chemist William Hyde Wollaston.

Rhodium occurs uncombined in nature and can be found in river sands in North and South America.

What contains rhodium?

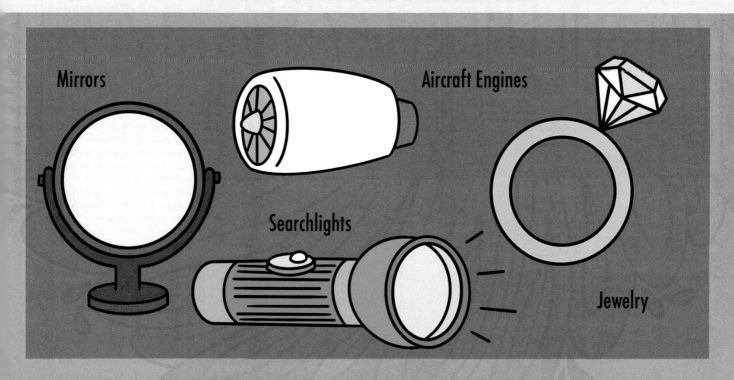

Iridium

Iridium is a chemical element and is a silvery-white and hard metal.

Iridium toxicity can cause cause irritation of the digestive tract and it may cause skin and eye irritations.

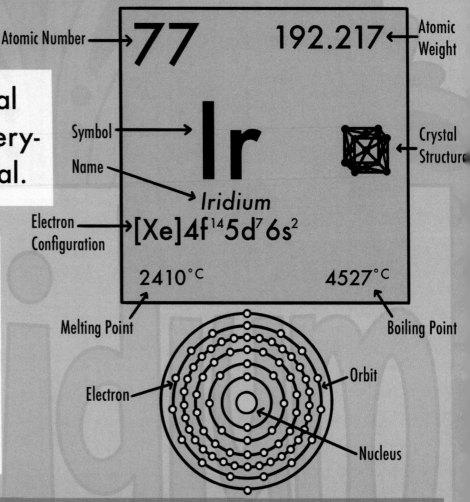

Atomic Number → 77

192.217 ← Atomic Weight

Symbol → Ir

Name → *Iridium*

Crystal Structure

Electron Configuration → $[Xe]4f^{14}5d^{7}6s^{2}$

2410°C

4527°C

Melting Point

Boiling Point

Electron

Orbit

Nucleus

It can be used as a hardening agent for platinum and it is also used to make devices needed for high temperatures. Iridium-192 is medically used as a source of gamma radiation for curing cancer with the application of Brachytherapy.

Iridium was discovered in 1803 by the English chemist Smithson Tennant.

Iridium is one of the rarest elements on Earth and is found uncombined in nature in sediments that were deposited by rivers.

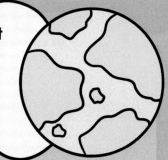

What contains iridium?

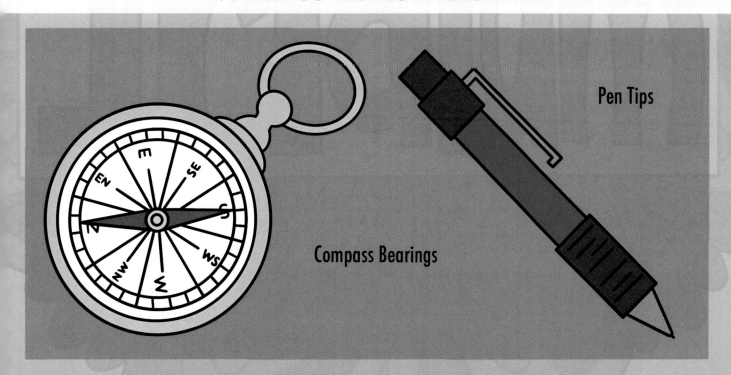

Compass Bearings

Pen Tips

Meitnerium

Meitnerium is a radioactive synthetic chemical element.

Meitnerium is expected to be harmful to living organisms because of its radioactivity.

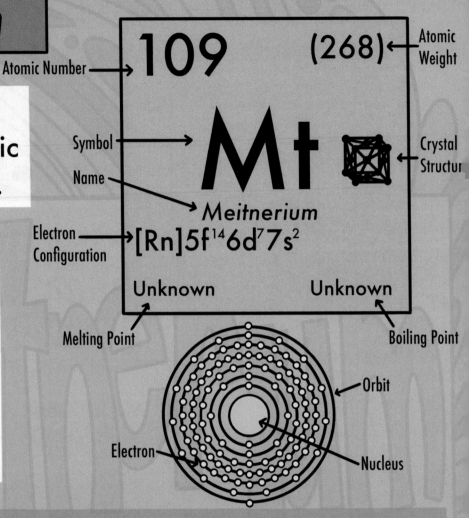

Atomic Number → 109

(268) ← Atomic Weight

Symbol → **Mt**

Crystal Structure

Name → *Meitnerium*

Electron Configuration → $[Rn]5f^{14}6d^{7}7s^{2}$

Unknown — Melting Point

Unknown — Boiling Point

Orbit

Electron

Nucleus

It is named after the Austrian physicist Lise Meitner who was born in Vienna in 1878. Meitnerium is created by bombarding atoms of bismuth-209 with ions of iron-58 with a device known as a linear accelerator.

Gottfried Münzenberg

Meitnerium was discovered in 1982 by the German physics Peter Armbruster and Gottfried Münzenberg.

Peter Armbruster

Meitnerium does not occur naturally on Earth and it is only produced in a lab.

What contains meitnerium?

Nothing

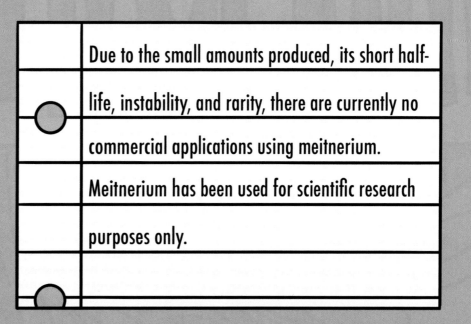

○	Due to the small amounts produced, its short half-life, instability, and rarity, there are currently no commercial applications using meitnerium.
	Meitnerium has been used for scientific research purposes only.
○	

Nickel

Nickel is a chemical element and is a silvery-white and lustrous metal.

Nickel toxicity can cause headaches, lung fibrosis, cardiovascular diseases, lung cancer, nasal cancer, and epigenetic effects.

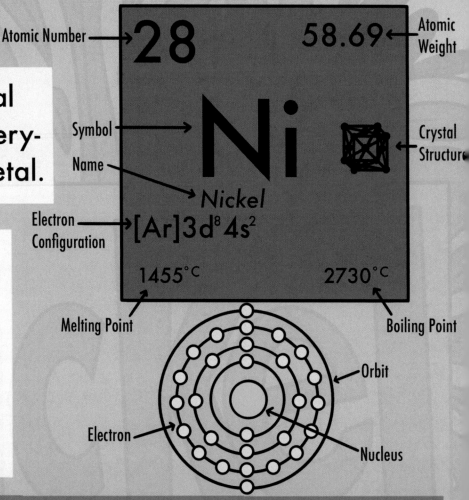

Atomic Number → **28**

58.69 ← Atomic Weight

Symbol → **Ni**

Crystal Structure

Name

Nickel

Electron Configuration → [Ar]3d^{8}4s^2

1455°C

2730°C

Melting Point

Boiling Point

Orbit

Electron

Nucleus

It can be used in gas turbines and rocket engines as it has the capability to resist corrosion even at high temperature. Nickel is medically used for preventing nickel levels in the blood from getting too low.

Nickel was discovered in 1751 by the Swedish chemist Axel Fredrik Cronstedt.

Nickel is naturally present in the Earth crust usually in combinations with oxygen and sulfur as oxides and sulfides.

What contains nickel?

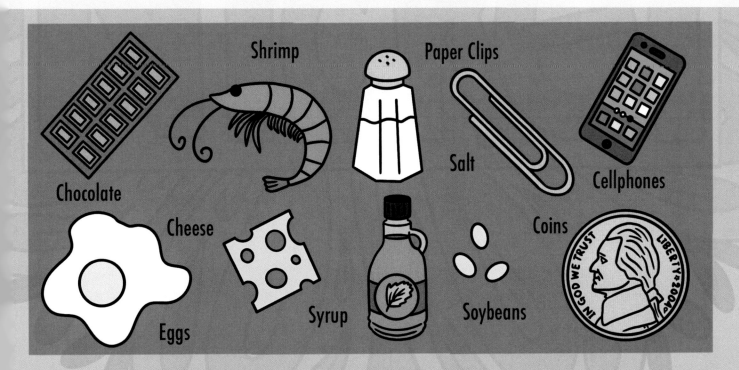

Chocolate

Shrimp

Paper Clips

Salt

Cellphones

Cheese

Coins

Eggs

Syrup

Soybeans

Palladium

Palladium is a chemical element and is a silver-white and lustrous metal.

Palladium toxicity can cause bone marrow, liver, and kidney damage. It also causes considerable damage and degradation of DNA.

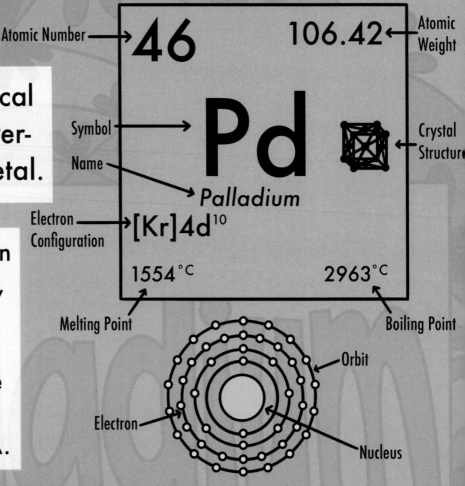

Atomic Number → 46

106.42 ← Atomic Weight

Symbol → **Pd**

Name → *Palladium*

Crystal Structure

Electron Configuration → [Kr]4d^{10}

1554°C

2963°C

Melting Point

Boiling Point

Orbit

Electron

Nucleus

It can be used in catalytic converters and it is a key component in emissions-reducing devices for cars and trucks. Palladium is medically used in the clinic for prostate cancer and choroidal melanoma brachytherapy.

Palladium was discovered in 1803 by the English chemist William Hyde Wollaston.

Palladium occurs uncombined in nature and can be found in sulfide minerals such as braggite.

What contains palladium?

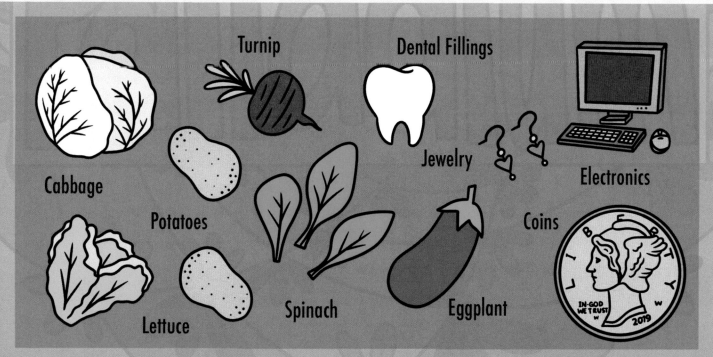

Cabbage

Turnip

Dental Fillings

Jewelry

Electronics

Potatoes

Coins

Lettuce

Spinach

Eggplant

Platinum

Platinum is a chemical element and is a silvery-white and metallic metal.

Platinum toxicity can cause kidney disease, muscle spasms, cancer, high blood pressure, and deafness.

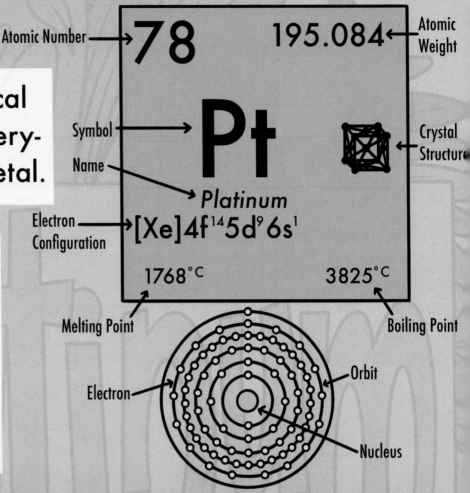

Atomic Number → 78

195.084 ← Atomic Weight

Symbol → **Pt**

Name → Platinum

Electron Configuration → [Xe]4f^{14}5d^{9}6s^{1}

Crystal Structure

1768°C

3825°C

Melting Point

Boiling Point

Electron

Orbit

Nucleus

It can be used in catalytic converters, laboratory equipment, electrical contacts and electrodes. Platinum is used in medical devices like pacemakers, implantable defibrillators, catheters, stents and neuromodulation devices.

Platinum was discovered in 1735 by the Spanish scientist Antonio de Ulloa.

Platinum occurs in nature as a pure metal and is commonly found in basic igneous rocks, such as peridotite and dunites.

What contains platinum?

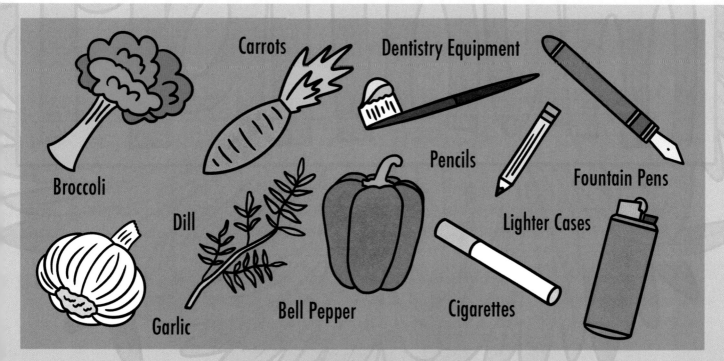

Broccoli

Carrots

Dentistry Equipment

Pencils

Fountain Pens

Dill

Lighter Cases

Garlic

Bell Pepper

Cigarettes

Darmstadtium

Darmstadtium is a radioactive synthetic chemical element.

Darmstadtium is expected to be harmful to living organisms because of its radioactivity.

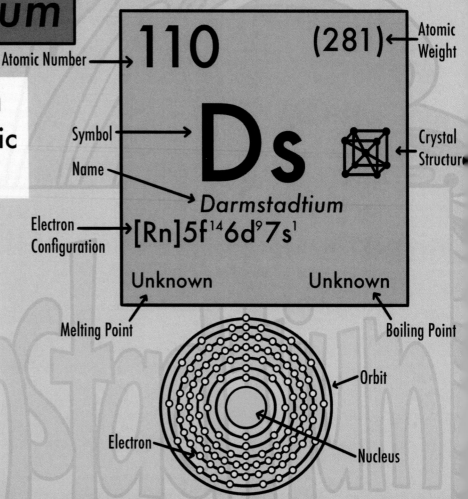

Atomic Number → 110

(281) ← Atomic Weight

Symbol → **Ds**

Crystal Structure →

Name → *Darmstadtium*

Electron Configuration → [Rn]5f^{14}6d^{9}7s^1

Unknown — Melting Point

Unknown — Boiling Point

Orbit

Electron

Nucleus

It is named after Darmstadt, Germany, which was where the element was first produced. Darmstadtium is created by bombarding lead^{-208} atoms with nickel^{-62} atoms in a heavy ion accelerator.

Darmstadtium was discovered in 1994 by the German physicist Sigurd Hofmann.

Darmstadtium does not occur naturally on Earth and it is only produced in a lab.

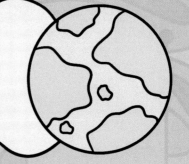

What contains darmstadtium?

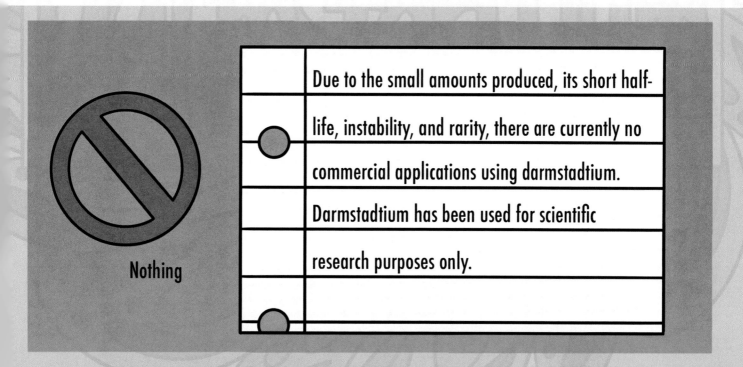

Nothing

○	Due to the small amounts produced, its short half-life, instability, and rarity, there are currently no commercial applications using darmstadtium.
	Darmstadtium has been used for scientific research purposes only.
○	

Copper

Copper is a chemical element and is a reddish orange and soft metal.

Copper toxicity can cause headaches, fever, diarrhea, liver damage, heart failure, brain damage, rheumatoid arthritis, and hepatitis.

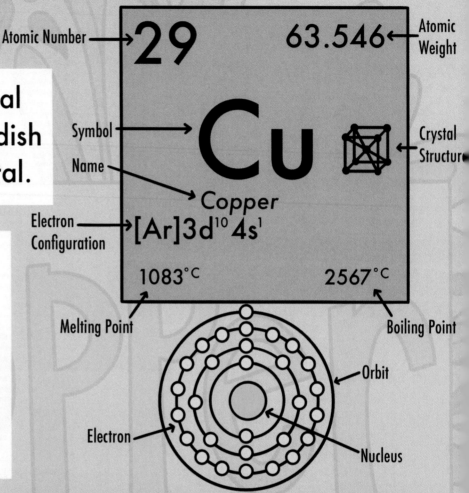

Atomic Number → 29   63.546 ← Atomic Weight

Symbol → Cu ← Crystal Structure

Name → Copper

Electron Configuration → [Ar]3d^{10} 4s^1

1083°C   2567°C

Melting Point   Boiling Point

Orbit

Electron

Nucleus

It can be used in building construction, power generation, electronic product manufacturing, and the production of industrial machinery. Copper is medically used for Alzheimer disease, acne, and tooth plaque.

Copper was discovered around 9000 BCE by the Sumerians living in ancient Mesopotamia.

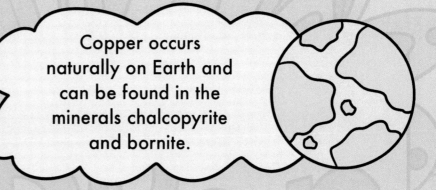

Copper occurs naturally on Earth and can be found in the minerals chalcopyrite and bornite.

What contains copper?

Pears

Almonds

Microwaves

Cauliflower

Refrigerators

Bananas

Trumpets

Beer

Pasta

Lima Beans

Silver

Silver is a chemical element and is a shiny white and lustrous metal.

Silver toxicity exhibits low toxicity in the human body and is not known to cause cancer, reproductive or neurological damage.

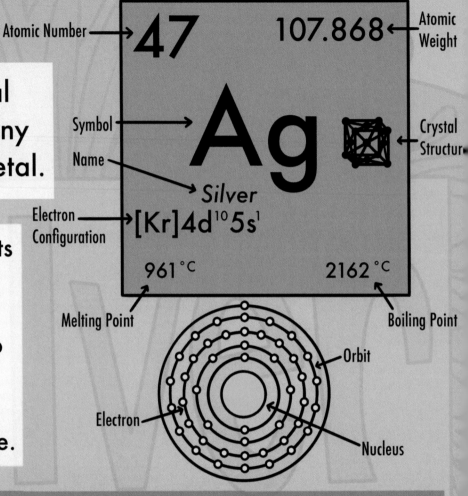

Atomic Number → 47

107.868 ← Atomic Weight

Symbol → Ag

← Crystal Structure

Name

Silver

Electron Configuration → [Kr]4d^{10}5s^1

961°C

2162°C

Melting Point

Boiling Point

Orbit

Electron

Nucleus

It can be used in dental alloys, solder and brazing alloys, electrical contacts and batteries. Silver is medically used in wound dressings, creams, and as an antibiotic coating on medical devices.

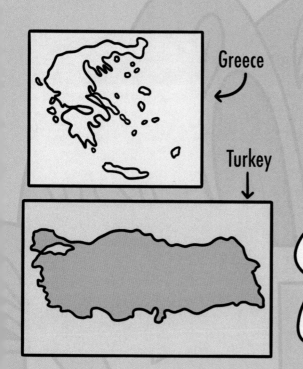

Greece

Turkey

Silver was discovered around 3000 BCE in Turkey and Greece.

Silver occurs naturally on Earth and it can also be found in other elements like sulfide, chloride and nitrate.

What contains silver?

Apples

Cucumbers

Sunburst Squash

Dishwashers

Air Conditioners

Lettuce

Cabbage

Grapes

Silverware

Cameras

Gold

Gold is a chemical element and is a bright, orange-yellow metal.

Gold toxicity may cause diarrhea, nausea, abdominal pain, vomiting, and shortness of breath.

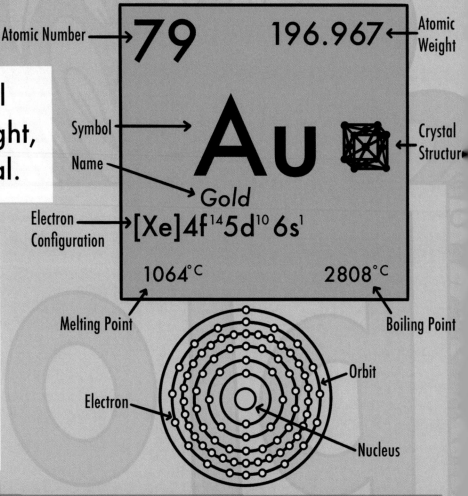

Atomic Number → 79

196.967 ← Atomic Weight

Symbol → Au

Crystal Structure

Name → Gold

Electron Configuration → [Xe]4f^{14}5d^{10}6s^{1}

1064°C

2808°C

Melting Point

Boiling Point

Orbit

Electron

Nucleus

It can be used in dentistry, medicine, aerospace, and it has been used to make ornamental objects and jewelry for thousands of years. Gold is medically used to treat juvenile rheumatoid arthritis and psoriatic arthritis.

Gold was discovered around 2600 BCE by the ancient Mesopotamians.

Gold is found deep in the layers of the Earth where it is transported by water, molten lava and volcanic eruptions, and earthquakes.

What contains gold?

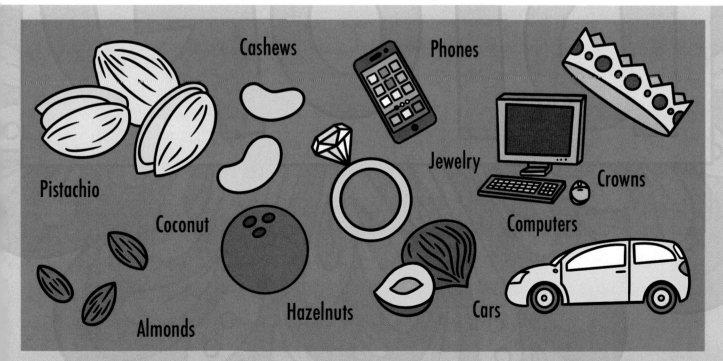

Pistachio

Cashews

Phones

Jewelry

Crowns

Computers

Coconut

Almonds

Hazelnuts

Cars

Roentgenium

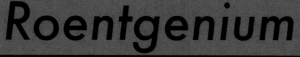

Roentgenium

Roentgenium is a radioactive synthetic chemical element.

Roentgenium is expected to be harmful to living organisms because of its radioactivity.

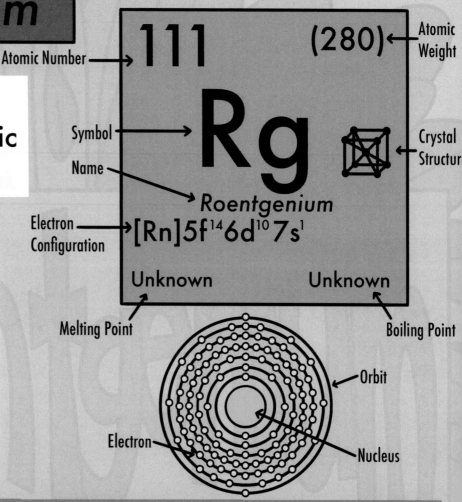

Atomic Number → 111

(280) ← Atomic Weight

Symbol → **Rg**

Crystal Structure

Name → *Roentgenium*

Electron Configuration → $[Rn]5f^{14}6d^{10}7s^1$

Unknown

Melting Point

Unknown

Boiling Point

Orbit

Electron

Nucleus

It is named after the German physicist Wilhelm Conrad Röntgen who was the discoverer of x-rays. Roentgenium is created by bombarding bismuth-209 with nickel-64 in a heavy ion accelerator.

Victor Ninov

Sigurd Hofmann

Roentgenium was discovered in 1994 by the German physicist Sigurd Hofmann and the Bulgarian physicist Victor Ninov.

Roentgenium does not occur naturally on Earth and it is only produced in a lab.

What contains roentgenium?

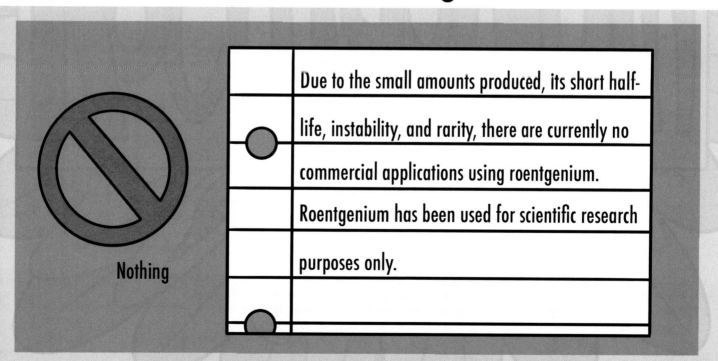

Nothing

- Due to the small amounts produced, its short half-life, instability, and rarity, there are currently no commercial applications using roentgenium. Roentgenium has been used for scientific research purposes only.

Zinc

Zinc is a chemical element and is a silvery-white and brittle metal.

Zinc toxicity can cause nausea, vomiting, stomachache, diarrhea, headaches, weakness, fever, muscle soreness, chest pain, and coughing.

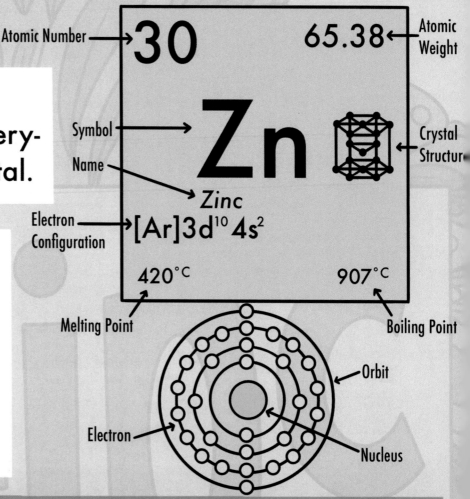

Atomic Number → **30**

65.38 ← Atomic Weight

Symbol → **Zn**

Name → Zinc

Crystal Structure

Electron Configuration → [Ar]3d^{10}4s^2

420°C

907°C

Melting Point

Boiling Point

Orbit

Electron

Nucleus

It can be used to to help with the common cold, lung infections, malaria, asthma, wound healing, ulcers, acne, and skin infections. Zinc can also be used to help with age-related problems like macular degeneration or Alzheimer disease.

Zinc was discovered in 1746 by the German chemist Andreas Sigismund Marggraf.

Zinc is not found in its pure elemental form, but is found in minerals in the Earth's crust.

What contains zinc?

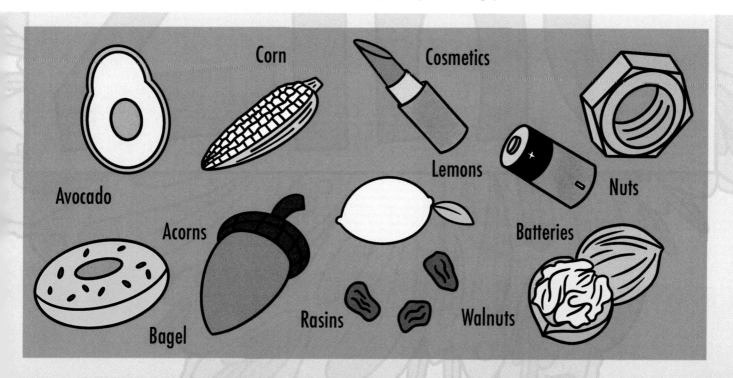

Cadmium

Cadmium is a chemical element and is a silver-white and soft metal.

Cadmium toxicity can cause nausea, diarrhea, vomiting, abdominal pain, cramping, coughing, chest pain, and flu like symptoms.

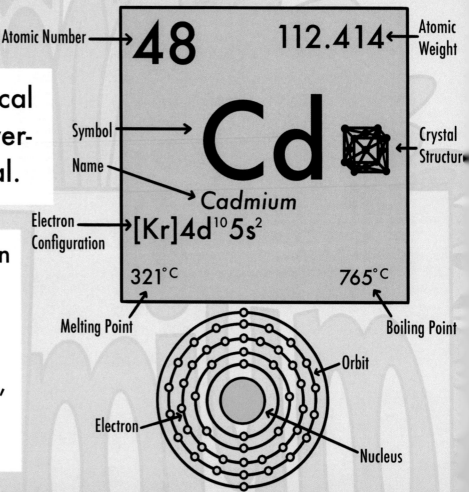

Atomic Number → 48

112.414 ← Atomic Weight

Symbol → Cd

Crystal Structure

Name → Cadmium

Electron Configuration → $[Kr]4d^{10}5s^2$

321°C

765°C

Melting Point

Boiling Point

Orbit

Electron

Nucleus

It can be used in in batteries, alloys, coatings (electroplating), solar cells, plastic stabilizers, and pigments. Cadmium iodide was used as a medication to treat enlarged joints, scrofulous glands, and chilblains.

Friedrich Stromeyer

Karl Hermann

Cadmium was discovered in 1817 by the German chemists Karl Hermann and Friedrich Stromeyer.

Cadmium found naturally in the Earth's crust and is often found in small quantities in zinc ores, such as sphalerite.

What contains cadmium?

Broccoli

Carrots

Pumpkins

Cashews

Paints

Brazil Nuts

Ceramics

Apple

Garlic

Cucumbers

Mercury

Mercury is a chemical element and is a silver-white and shiny metal.

Mercury toxicity can cause muscle weakness, nausea, vomiting, difficulty breathing, and changes in vision, hearing, or speech.

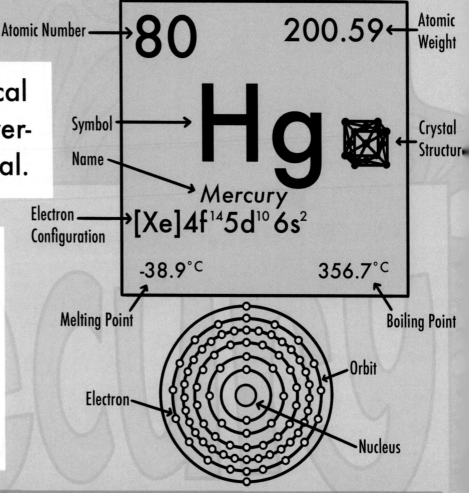

Atomic Number → **80**

200.59 ← Atomic Weight

Symbol → **Hg**

← Crystal Structure

Name → Mercury

Electron Configuration → $[Xe]4f^{14}5d^{10}6s^2$

-38.9°C

356.7°C

Melting Point

Boiling Point

Orbit

Electron

Nucleus

It can be used in many scientific instruments such as thermometers and barometers and its electrical conductivity it is used to make silent switches. Mercury is medically used in worming medications and teething powders.

Ida Noddack

Walter Noddack

Otto Berg

Mercury was known to the ancient Chinese and Hindus. It was found in Egyptian tombs that date from 1500 BC.

Mercury rarely occurs uncombined in nature and is found mainly in cinnabar ores.

What contains mercury?

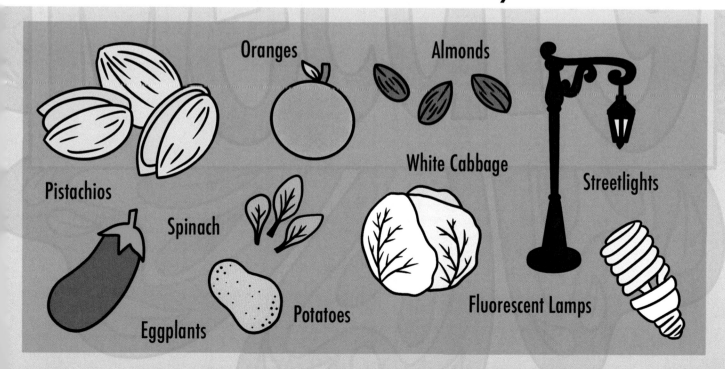

Pistachios

Oranges

Almonds

White Cabbage

Streetlights

Spinach

Eggplants

Potatoes

Fluorescent Lamps

Copernicium

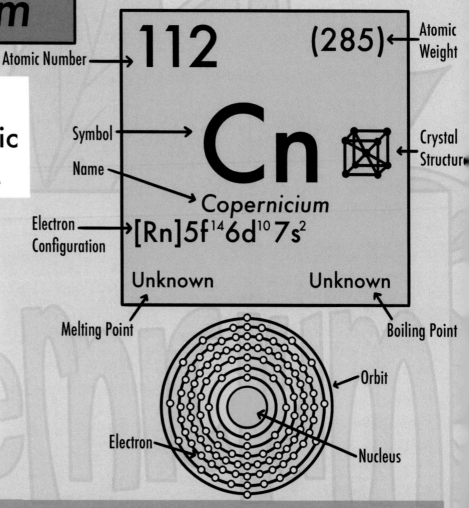

Atomic Number → **112**

(285) ← Atomic Weight

Symbol → **Cn**

Name → *Copernicium*

Crystal Structure

Electron Configuration → $[Rn]5f^{14}6d^{10}7s^2$

Unknown — Melting Point

Unknown — Boiling Point

Orbit

Electron

Nucleus

Copernicium is a radioactive synthetic chemical element.

Copernicium is expected to be harmful to living organisms because of its radioactivity.

It is named after Nicolaus Copernicus who was an influential 16th century astronomer. Copernicium is made by bombarding atoms of lead with ions of zinc through a linear accelerator.

Victor Ninov

Copernicium was discovered in 1996 by the German physicist Sigurd Hofmann and the Bulgarian physicist Victor Ninov.

Sigurd Hofmann

Copernicium does not occur naturally on Earth and it is only produced in a lab.

What contains copernicium?

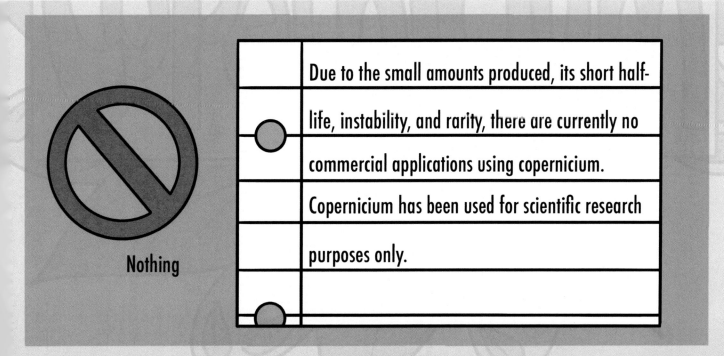

Nothing

- Due to the small amounts produced, its short half-life, instability, and rarity, there are currently no commercial applications using copernicium.
- Copernicium has been used for scientific research purposes only.

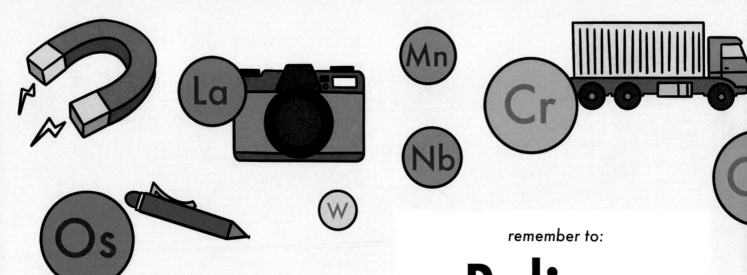

The End!

remember to:

Believe
Dream
Achieve

More Bearific® books on bearific.com

Katelyn Lonas

Cd	Hg	Zn
Cadmium	Mercury	Zinc
112.414	200.592	65.38
72	41	26
Hf	Nb	Fe
Hafnium	Niobium	Iron
178.49	92.906	55.845

Katelyn is a 15 year old who resides in Southern California. Katelyn loves to encourage others to always believe in themselves and chase after their dreams! She started writing and illustrating her first book at age 9 and then published 53 more books. She hopes you enjoy reading this book and be ready for more books to come!

80	30
Hg	Zn
Mercury	Zinc
200.592	65.38
41	26
Nb	Fe
Niobium	Iron

-Katelyn

38	112.414	200.592	65.38	112.414	200.592

6	72	41	26	72	41
e	Hf	Nb	Fe	Hf	Nb
on	Hafnium	Niobium	Iron	Hafnium	Niobium
845	178.49	92.906	55.845	178.49	92.906

0	48	80	30	48	80
n	Cd	Hg	Zn	Cd	Hg
nc	Cadmium	Mercury	Zinc	Cadmium	Mercur
38	112.414	200.592	65.38	112.414	200.59

6	72	41	26	72	41
e	Hf	Nb	Fe	Hf	Nb
on	Hafnium	Niobium	Iron	Hafnium	Niobium
845	178.49	92.906	55.845	178.49	92.90

0	48	80	30	48	80
n	Cd	Hg	Zn	Cd	Hg
nc	Cadmium	Mercury	Zinc	Cadmium	Mercur
38	112.414	200.592	65.38	112.414	200.59

6	72	41	26	72	41
e	Hf	Nb	Fe	Hf	Nb